View of part of the town

The Cuatro Postes

CAMILO JOSÉ CELA

AVILA

EDITORIAL NOGUER, S. A.

BARCELONA - MADRID

English translation by
JOHN FORRESTER

Photographs by
CIGANOVIC, FOAT, ARCHIVO MAS, F. CATALÁ ROCA and SALMER

914,6
CEa

7 th. EDITION revised and enlarged - 1974
RESERVED IN ALL COUNTRIES
© by EDITORIAL NOGUER, S.A. 1974
Paseo de Gracia, 96 - Barcelona
I.S.B.N. 84-279-8323-9
Depósito Legal: B. 39.320-73
Colour: Industrias Gráficas F. Casamajó - Barcelona
Text printed by Romargraf, S.A.- Sants, 387 - Barcelona
Printed in Spain

CONTENTS

The soul and mind of Avila 7

Avilesian itineraries 9

    General itinerary 10

    In the steps of Santa Teresa 19

Some suggestions for the excursionist 23

    First journey 24

    Second excursion 24

    Third trip 25

Avila - Mediaeval bazaar. Craftsmanship 26

The Avilesian cuisine. 28

The Avilesian character, local customs and traditional fiestas. 30

Practical information supplement

Convent of las Madres

Convent of Santo Tomás

THE SOUL AND MIND OF AVILA

Avila, 1127 metres above sea level, the Spanish city that lives nearest to Heaven is a tiny, peaceful city, walled and gentle, withdrawn, noble and quiet. Perhaps for the tourist Avila might have the virtue of making him understand Castile without needing to go outside its walls. Avila is somehow the essence of Castile, its living spirit. Everything Castile has, strange and surprising, unusual and awesome, can be found concentrated in Avila. Old Castile —New Castile would need another interpretation of its people, its soul and its landscape— is a very hard yet delicate world, like a diamond, difficult to discover, sparkling easily but taking a long time to show its heart. Among all the cities of Castile Avila is perhaps the most Castilian, that one in which the forms and facets that make *lo castellano* show themselves to the material and spiritual eye. Avila has no square like that of Salamanca nor a cathedral like that of León or Burgos, neither has she a fortress like that of Segovia, nor archives such as has Simancas, but Avila nevertheless concentrates the essence of Castile in the limpid air which she breathes

7

and which envelopes her; she has an indefinable and winged something that yet marks her personality as surely as a branding iron marks a bull. Looking through half-closed eyes at Avila it is not difficult for the tourist to imagine himself in the Middle Ages, to touch the coldness of mediaeval times, to feel their longings, their preoccupations and their mystical military and artisan pulsations. Those chiselled faces, those keen, steely eyes, the thick Castilian noses, translucent foreheads and ashen hair can still be seen in the streets, in the squares and under the porches of Avila, like details discovered in old museums.

History

Historically, Avila stands forth somewhat confused. Her origins are uncertain and the fact of seeing in geography books the same name several times, inside and outside of Spain, casts new shades over what already could not be seen clearly. The Celtiberians, during their stay in our city, left their imprint in the sculptures of bulls and pigs which can still be admired in the interior of the noble patios, near the old mansions and even on its streets and squares. The Romans built up a colony in Avila, probably of a military character, their traces are numerous and the presence of the symbolic fish of the Christian Romans makes us suppose that their dominion lasted many years. Te arrival of Bishop San Segundo, patron of the city and one of the seven Apostolic Varons is supposed to have taken place in this epoch (1st century); this event is still doubted in spite of the discovery of a sepulchre supposed to be that of the Saint in the church of San Sebastián in 1519, from then on called the Hermitage of San Segundo. Lope de Vega wrote a play in which he describes the excitement in the village over the discovery. During the Visigoth and Arab occupations Avila is supposed, by some historians, to have been a city of strong walls and prosperous life for which both parties fought hard. It is better not to have too much faith in all concrete assertions made about that epoch. The most probable thing is that Visigothic Avila had at that time a languid and precarious life and that the city, abandoned before the Arab avalanche, was never permanently occupied. The fact that the 11th century Walls, probably built with stone found at hand, show Celtiberian and Roman traces, but lack Visigoth and Arab imprints can be considered as symptomatic. Alfonso VI, after the reconquest of Toledo in 1085, erected a second defence line commanded by don Raimundo de Borgoña, which supported him, among other probable places, in Segovia, Avila and Salamanca. It is since this moment that Avila can be considered as Avila itself; five years later the building of the Walls began. Uninhabited Avila was then populated by people from the North —Galicia, Asturias, Santander, León and Burgos— and soon the city returned to life again from its ruins and started to become important in the history of Spain. The population of Avila was divided into two big groups —noblemen and plebeians— and from the good understanding between them the military virtues were born which were to become the permanent characteristic of the city. The first military enterprise of the people of Avila took place in 1105 when under Sancho Sánchez Zurraquín —who died the following year during the conquest of Cuenca— they defeated the Arabs in Zaragoza. We cite only this one action, as the enumeration of the military enterprises undertaken by Avila would take us far from our subject. Historically, it is thought that the legendary Nalvillos, a brave fighter whose men proclaimed him King, appeared about this time. An important figure in the life of Avila —a city which has a lct of important figures among its folk— was Alonso Tostado Ribera or Alonso de Madrigal, author of several books and Bishop in 1449, who was so small that it is said Pope Eugenio IV, supposing he was on his knees, told him to get up. The expulsion of the Arabs, which coincided with the exodus of the nobles towards the Court, was a hard blow to Avila, whose population was reduced to something over one thousand five hundred people. Santa Teresa de Jesús is perhaps the most remarkable figure in the whole history of Avila. We talk about the memories of her in the city in another part of this brief guide. During the War of Independence Avila organised a regiment of volunteers who fought heroically in Ciudad-Rodrigo. From that day to this, Avila, mystic and traditional, honest and strong, waits patiently for the friendly heart to whom to give her mysterious secret.

AVILESIAN ITINERARIES

The tourist, when reaching any city, needs two things: a bar where he can enjoy a drink and a Post Office, to get in touch with his family. Let us begin our itineraries of Avila from the *plaza de Santa Teresa de Jesús*. Arrive in Avila by whatever means you prefer, the *plaza de Santa Teresa* is the centre of the city and the most suitable rendez-vous. There we can find

9

bars, the shops, souvenir and picture postcard kiosks and on the nearby Plaza de la Catedral, the General Post Office.

We are already in the *plaza de Santa Teresa*. We have had our breakfast —we imagine it is in the morning— we have already wired or written to our family and are ready to visit the city.

We are going to trace two itineraries for the visitor. The first a general one and the second in the steps of Santa Teresa, although we shall find in the latter monuments which bear no reference to the Saint. We shall follow both on foot. Avila is as tiny as a pocket handkerchief, moreover the withdrawn dreamy spirit of the city is apt to pass unnoticed by the tourist who wants to go everywhere by car.

How long will each itinerary take us? The question must remain unanswered. If we want no more than an impression of the city each itinerary may last a day or perhaps less. If our purpose is to go deeply into the mystery of Avila, to go far into its quiet charm, to dig into its history and architecture, perhaps we will need more than a year of daily work.

Let us suppose that the reader wants to "know" but not to "study" Avila.

General itinerary

We go into the walled enclosure through the stout PUERTA DEL ALCÁZAR, about which we shall talk in detail when we refer to the Walls. By the first lane on the right we reach, after turning two corners, the *plaza de la* CATEDRAL. Before admiring its façade and before entering to examine the interior, because it will take us a long time, let us look at the CASA DE VALDERRÁBANOS or DE GONZALO DÁVILA, whose twin arched windows, 15th century entrance, and heraldries, given to Gonzalo Dávila during the conquest of Gibraltar (1462), have great interest. The stone watchdogs with human faces, had arses about which jokes of every kind were made: to which the owner put an end by ordering that the unfortunate animals be mutilated.

The Cathedral
The CATHEDRAL, on our left while we were looking at the *Casa de Valderrábanos*, is a wonderful and curious fortified temple whose age it is difficult to state with accuracy. Some authors

10

The Cathedral

The Cathedral. The naves

assert that the construction took place from 1091 to 1107 according to a project by Alvar García, and others assure us that it was the work of Maestro Fruchel, who died at the end of the 12th century; the most probable thing is that the work took place a short time afterwards and it is the result of the cooperation of several architects and possibly also of some prelate who lent a hand in the building. Perhaps the towers and the *main chapel* are 12th century works; the first part of the towers and the first and second naves are 13th century and the rest, the second part of the towers, the cloisters and the vaults, 14th century. The style is Romanesque in transition to gothic, all in the French way, although we can observe English details. The Cathedral can be considered a perfect fortress with its high, fortified East tower, its three battlements, two parapets, covered gallery and the drill square; it also has a military door on the West set in two crenellated towers and a double line of battlements on the North and South, today half ruined; in the precincts there was a spring in case of siege. During the 16th century the Cathedral lost its double military and ecclesiastic character in order to avoid the frequent territorial disputes this had occasioned.

The Exterior

The façade we now see is the West one; it would be more beautiful if it were less confused, but it shows the results of the unfortunate reforms of the 18th century; of the two flanking towers one remained unfinished. The wonderful *porch of the Apostles* was on this façade till the 15th century. Today we can admire this 13th century masterpiece on the North façade. This porch widens in a carpanel arch at whose point is an image of the Saviour; these elements, as well as the cresting and ornaments, date from the time of its removal. The porch, so called, consists of five pointed tympan vaulted arches, sculptured with symbolic scenes and twelve finely proportioned Apostles with musical instruments. The two figures in the foreground are, probably, the oldest. On the left of the porch there is still a fragment of the romanesque wall, which ends in the artificial neoclassic *chapel by Velada*; and on the right we see an uninteresting Renaissance addition. Each façade we have talked of has a pair of chained lions added in the 18th century. The view of the South façade is spoilt by some buildings, which have no interest other than anecdotal; we can notice the stout walls of the cloisters provided with solid buttresses and ending in graceful cresting, a work of Pedro de Viniegra and Vasco de

Zarza; *a medallion* with a bust of a woman, LIFE, and *another* with a skull, DEATH, gives the name to the typical little street in which we stand. The East façade holds as main characteristic its apse with triple crenelated parapet and the chapel of San Segundo.

The Interior

We have already admired the outside of the Cathedral; now we shall go inside for a short visit, only giving attention to the most remarkable things. This cruciform edifice has three naves, a transept, double apse-aisle, cloisters, sacristy and ante-sacristy, chapter hall and several chapels which were added through the years. Te columns are in Cluniacensian style and the vaults are similar to those of Rheims. There are still interesting glass windows from the 15th and 16th centuries, which perhaps survived the earthquake in the 18th century; those of the North gallery deserve special attention. This temple is very interesting for its *tombs*, which are not yet well identified and listed. In the half light of the interior of the West door, we see two wonderful sculptures of the 15th century by Juan Guas. The rich velvet 15th century curtains which adorned the main nave were sold to a ragman! The *main chapel* —in sandstone from this regions— is in Roman style and on its windows we notice certain Arabic signs; the 15th century tomb of Bishop Roelas, worthy of mention, is in alabaster and after the Burgundian school. We must give special attention to the wonderful *retable*, a true jewel among the first Spanish paintings, composed of twenty-four lovely panels by Berruguete, Borgoña and Santa Cruz; its frame is a work by Vasco de Zarza as is the alabaster *Monstrance*. The door in silver relief is attributed to García Crespo, a silversmith from Salamanca in the 18th century. In the apse-aisle we find the great *sepulchre of Tostado*, a masterpeice of plateresque [1] in alabaster, also by Zarza; the polychrome tombstone of the first sepulchre is very curious. The *choir-stalls*, a work by Cornelis de Holanda (16th century) are also in plateresque style and have a solid construction; the capricious decoration of the *choir* is as beautiful as it is original. *Behind the choir*, the capitals and the bizarre form of the plinth are remarkable. The plateresque *altars of San Segundo* and of *Santa Catalina* are beautifully executed. The *pulpit of the Epistle*, in ogival style, is a work by Llorente de Avila (1520) and that *of the Gospel*, also plateresque, is attributed

[1] Plateresque: a delicate ornate architectural decoration used in Spain in the 16th century.

12

to the same artist. The *font* would seem to date from the beginning of the 15th century; the decoration in the hemicycle is by Zarza. In the ancient atrium we find the *chapels of San Andrés* and *San Miguel*. Among other sepulchres we see there the famous tomb of the noble Esteban Domingo, founder of one of the two lineages of the city. In the *chapel of San Juan Evangelista* the gothic tombs of Bishop Domingo Xuárez and of doña Beatriz Básquez are to be found. The two oldest shrines of the Cathedral are that of *Bishop don Sancho* (12th century) and that of a *choirmaster, don Tacón* (13th century). These can be noticed in the Chapel of *Nuestra Señora de Gracia*. It is possible to admire the beautiful retable of San Isidro Villaldo (1551) in the *chapel of San Antolín*. The *chapel of San Segundo*, annexed to the temple, must be particularly remarked on because it was Lope de Vega's oratory from 1626 until his death. We enter the *cloister* through an ogival door in which we notice a curious San Cristobalón from the 13th century; on the walls there were formerly paintings by Sansón Florentino, which are now in the Cathedral Museum, and from the garden rises enchantment and an agreeable melancholy. In the *chapel of Christ* we must notice the wrought iron grill. In the *Sacristy* or *chapel of San Bernabé* we can admire an important alabaster retable. According to tradition, in this sacristy —then a chapter hall— the Comuneros once assembled, and later the noble people of Castile also met there to offer to Isabel la Católica the crown of Enrique IV. The museum is very modern and contains mementoes of great value, particularly noteworthy being the great custody made by Juan de Arfe; the library, once of a certain value, was sacked by the State in 1869.

Casa de Velada
We have already taken a quick glance at the Cathedral and here we are in the street again. With our backs to the door which we went through when we entered we notice, on the right, just at the corner of *plaza del Tostado* and *calle del Tostado*, the CASA DE VELADA with its wonderful stone-work tower and its noble shields supported by lion's heads. We ought to pay special attention to the façade towards *calle del Tostado*. At the other end of the square is the PUERTA DE LOS LEALES or DEL PESO DE LA HARINA, of which we will talk when we speak about the Walls in general.

Casa de los Verdugo
Going along *calle del Tostado* as far as PUERTA DE SAN VICENTE

13

we find in the *calle de Lope Núñez* the CASA DE LOS VERDUGO on the left, a mysterious house and one of the best preserved buildings in the city; it has two towers and a shield resting on an eagle with its wings spread. The door is decorated with the girdle of San Francisco and beside one of the towers we can contemplate a magnificent Celtiberian bull carved in stone.

Church of San Vicente

Proceeding by PUERTA DE SAN VICENTE we reach the church of the same name, worthy of a careful visit. The CHURCH OF SAN VICENTE, according to an old legend, was built by a Jew in whom a curious miracle was worked. During the year 306 the Gentiles cruelly killed three Christian brothers, Vicente, Sabina and Cristeta, afterwards abandoning their bodies in the open to be devoured by beasts. From the first moment the bodies were defended by a snake that kept away any live being. A Jew approaching the scene to mock the corpses, was attacked by the snake which twisted itself round his neck till, moved by his experience, the Jew was converted to the Christian faith. He ordered a temple to be built to the memory of the martyrs and together with those of San Marcos de León and Santa Gadea de Burgos, it was one of the three most important adjuration churches in Castile. The romanic church of San Vicente, built almost entirely of sandstone from La Colilla, shows on its South façade, in addition to some curious images, the most beautiful and important cornice known (it could only be compared, although at a distance, with that of the apse of Tarragona Cathedral and with that of *Notre-Dame la Grande* of Poitiers). It is composed of two hundred and seven elements and its figures represent the fight of MORAL CORRUPTION against VIRTUE. The West façade also, with its pointed arch, its porch reminding us of the famous one of the *Gloria* of Santiago de Compostela and its two towers, has great beauty; the other two façades, although they too are important, have not the same grandeur. The inside of the basílica, airy and well proportioned, has a true artistic interest if we do not give much importance to some unfortunate restorations. The tomb of SS. Vicente, Sabina, and Cristeta, possibly the work of Fruchel, contains some remarkable reliefs.

Church of San Andrés

Behind the North façade, leaving the road from Villacastín to Vigo, and taking either *calle de Parrilla* or *calle de Valseca* we reach the CHURCH OF SAN ANDRÉS. It is a less important building,

14

The Cathedral.
The main altar

Convent of Santa Teresa

also built in golden sandstone, but in it the genuine romanic style is conserved; inside, the capitals of the triumphal arch are outstanding, they are a curious construction. Today this church is shut for worship; recently, it has been restored carefully. From the *plaza San Andrés*, along *calle de Ajates*, we arrive at the road from Villacastín to Vigo again; from here we will start a lengthy walk around the WALLS.

Hermitages of San Martín and Nuestra Señora de la Cabeza

But before —and after having walked along the whole of *calle de Ajates*— we will stop for a while at the *hermitages of San Martín and Nuestra Señora de la Cabeza*. The mudéjar 14th century tower of the HERMITAGE OF SAN MARTÍN draws our attention; the rest of the building is 16th century and has been restored. That of NUESTRA SEÑORA DE LA CABEZA, attached for years to the *Cofradía de Escribanos*, was a place where mad people went looking for spiritual cure. It is suposed it was once a Moorish sanctuary, probably built in the 13th century.

Hermitage of San Segundo

In the North Western angle of the city, between the River Adaja and the Walls, is found the HERMITAGE OF SAN SEGUNDO —where the supposed remains of the Saint were found in 1519— a modest 12th century building, having three apses, a bell-gable and a wooden roof. The *sepulchre of the Saint* is the most remarkable thing in the hermitage, being of alabaster and dating from the beginning of the 16th century; it is one of the most beautiful works executed by the sculptor Juan de Juni; according to a remote tradition the Saint grants any favour one may ask him, if one puts one's own handkerchief into his tomb. Besides *San Segundo's* tomb we see that of *Santa Barbada*. This girl, in order to keep her virtue, asked God to destroy her beauty and in answer to her petition a beard slowly covered her beautiful maidenly face; this legend, which can hardly be credited, reminds us of that of *la Bella Mallorquina*, of Lulio. Perhaps we could impute most of the stories of this place to a conceited archpriest who, it seems, once officiated here. It is probable that the majority of them are due to his fantastic imagination, and have been handed down by word of mouth.

The Walls

After visiting the Hermitage of San Segundo we shall stop before the WALLS, which we have in fact been seeing for sometime. The spot where we are is perhaps the best one to see the Walls in grand perspective. We did not pay much attention to the WALLS when we found them during our tour, because we thought it better to consider them as a "whole". The huge Walls of Avila are, without any doubt, the oldest and best kept ones in Christendom. They are 11th century and are a work of those masters in "geometrical design" Casandro and Florín de Pituenga; Alvar García continued the work at a later date. Bishop don Pelayo blessed the foundation on May 3rd, 1090. The work of construction only lasted nine years and it is supposed that about two thousand workers were employed (those engaged on the building being perhaps conquered Moors). The perimeter is 2,5 Km round and has ninety towers, romanic in style with some Moorish influence. In the first part one can see latter day restorations and modifications, above all, those executed in the 14th century. The Walls form a trapezium and have NINE GATES, all of them very interesting and some having great beauty. We started our visit entering through the PUERTA DEL ALCÁZAR which is flanked by two solid towers where bloody fighting took place; the doorway has been restored —after the model of that of SAN VICENTE— but not very cleverly. We go out of the walled enclosure through the *Puerta de San Vicente,* to contemplate the church of the same name. This door was restored in 1517, when the typical diamond shaped merlons of these Walls were changed for others in brick work which we can see today. They were the model for those of the *Puerta del Alcázar.* In the East we find the PUERTA DE LOS LEALES or DEL PESO DE LA HARINA, where once there was the *Postigo de los Abates,* a 16th century work. To the North there is first, the PUERTA DEL MARISCAL, so called, because of its proximity to the house of the Mariscal de Castilla, don Alvaro Dávila, this is the only one which still has its original form, in the previous style to the ogival. Next we find the PUERTA DEL CARMEN, which breaks the line of the Walls according to the Arab habit. On the West we have the PUERTA DEL PUENTE or ARCO DE SAN SEGUNDO, restored during the 15th century, and finally we find on the south the PUERTA DE LA MALA VENTURA, simple and full of sad memories; it is said that those hostages burnt in Las Hervencias by Alonso de Aragón came out through this door. Then we reach the PUERTA DE MONTENEGRO or DE SANTA TERESA —near the place where her parents lived— with its square towers and machicolated gallery. Finally we come to the PUERTA DEL GRAJAL, DE LA ESTRELLA or DEL RASTRO with its huge carpanel arch. In the Walls there are still several remains from Celtiberian

Convent of Santo Tomás.
The cloister

The tower of the Casa de
los Guzmanes

Casa de Polentinos.
The courtyard

Convent of Santo Tomás.
A detail of the main
retable, by Berruguete

The walls

The Puerta del Alcázar

The street of Life and
Death

and Roman times which were included —or shall we say reco-vered— during its building.

The Cuatro Postes and the Convento de Santa Teresa

Continuing round the WALLS, after passing the CUATRO POSTES from where we can admire a beautiful view of the city, we enter the enclosure again through the *Puerta de Santa Teresa*. In the *plaza de la Santa* —we must not confuse this square with the *plaza de Santa Teresa de Jesús* where we started our tour— on the left, where we enter, there is the CASA DEL VIRREY DEL PERÚ, BLASCO NÚÑEZ VELA, a solid and original edifice, sensibly con-structed. In the same square, in front of the *Puerta*, there is the CONVENTO DE SANTA TERESA, built on the very grounds of the Cepeda, its style is baroque with some Herrerian influence. Nei-ther the façade nor the image of the Saint is beautiful; the mo-dern memorial stones executed in marble and placed on either side are rather ugly. On the West front we can still see the very site of the garden where the Saint played in her childhood. Inside we must remark on the *chapel of the Saint* built in the room where she was born. In the church we can also notice the mag-nificent *Scourging of Christ* by Gregorio Hernández. The crucifix the Saint had in her hands at the moment of her death is kept in a *glass case*. Several other *relics of the Saint* can be seen in the convent.

Casas de Almarza y Superunda

Leaving the *plaza de la Santa* and proceeding towards *plaza de los Cepeda*, today *plaza del General Mola*, we find the CASAS DE ALMARZA Y SUPERUNDA. The CASA DE LOS ALMARZA, at the present time belonging to LAS SIERVAS, is in tertiary gothic style and has beautiful, rich decoration. The half point door and the shields on its façade give this building an undeniable charm. The CASA DE LOS CONDES DE SUPERUNDA has a wonderful Florentine air and a unique elegance.

Casa de los Guzmanes

In this *plaza de los Cepeda* there is the CASA DE LOS GUZMANES or DE OÑATE (16th century) in renaissance gothic style, with its huge square tower, its fine wrought-iron windows, its heraldic stone and an interior which has been very carefully preserved with good taste. Alfonso XII stayed in this building when he visited Avila in 1878. Not far from the Plaza de los Cepeda —in the calle Vallespín— is the CASA de Polentinos (mid 16th century).

17

The doorway and typical square Spanish courtyard are very interesting. Today it is occupied by the Academia de Intendencia.

Casas de los Dávila

On our way to *Puerta del Rastro* and going a little to the left towards *plaza de la Fruta*, also surnamed *de los Dávila*, we find the four CASAS DE LOS DÁVILA; two on the square itself and the other two on the *plazuela del Rastro*. The *plaza de la Fruta* is one of the most beautiful squares in the city. The two houses of *plaza de la Fruta* are 13th century with two 14th century doors set in half pointed arches. Above one of the doors, there is the shield of *Trece Roeles*, granted to Hernán Pérez Dávila, because he took the standard with the same heraldic device from the Moors. The *Trece Roeles* refer to the thirteen villages of the Subcaliphate. On the façade of plaza de la Fruta and in the cornice of a huge window we can read, after the 16th century masters' names, the following: "where a door shuts, another opens". The last house in *plazuela del Rastro* is 13th century; the doors and the motifs used in their ornamentation are very beautiful. Close to the Walls, through *Puerta del Rastro*, leaving on the right the popular suburbs of the city, we find the *plaza de Santa Teresa*.

Church of San Pedro

In the same square, in one of the four corners, the one opposite where we are entering —we cannot get lost— there is the IGLESIA DE SAN PEDRO, the oldest church in the city. The *principal front,* that looking towards *plaza Santa Teresa*, also called *plaza del Alcázar* and *plaza del Mercado Grande*, consists of a curious porch with archivaults bounded by two stout buttresses, and one magnificent rose window decorated with archivaults. On the North façade we can admire the wonderful porch whose columns have capitals of a very complicated pattern and archivaults decorated with flower motifs and strange geometrical groupings. After the two façades we have already seen there is the atrium with 16th century lions; in this atrium Queen Isabel la Católica gave her oath to respect the *Fueros de Ávila*. The East front has three apses, some half pointed windows and a simple but curious cornice. The interior, steeped in a pleasant half light has an undeniable beauty, but we shall not tarry over its description at the moment. Our first trip is over.

Hermitage of San Segundo
Statue of the Saint, by
Juan de Juni

The Law Courts

In the steps of Santa Teresa

This itinerary will be briefer than the first because our companion might feel somewhat tired and in addition we have almost seen everything of Avila, this tiny, captivating city. Let us go back to the Walls, but this second visit will be rather in the nature of an opportunity for hearing old legends regarding the Saint's life and work among he old stones which saw her birth.

It would not be worth while following either a logical or a chronological trail about Santa Teresa's life on her native soil, as this would be tiring for the curious tourist, taking him from one place to another and back again after the Saint's memories. We must not forget that in walking about the city and the surrounding countryside Santa Teresa acquired her deepest fervour.

The method we are going to follow is quite simple and like that of the general itinerary: walking along the streets of Avila and stopping before the most important reminders of the Saint. On the other hand our companion —and friend— has already seen most of the places we are going to visit, so that with a little memory and with what he is going to see and read, it will be quite easy for him, to trace Teresa de Cepeda's life in Avila. Let us start off again, though we will not stop at those buildings and corners we have already seen.

Convento de Nuestra Señora de Gracia
Leaving the *Iglesia de San Pedro* on the left and after having walked about a hundred paces we come to the CONVENTO DE NUESTRA SEÑORA DE GRACIA, a simple 16th century building where Santa Teresa began her education under the care of Sor María Briceño when she was 17; it is worth while looking at the retable of the *main chapel*, a work by Juan Rodríguez and Lucas Giraldo. The present sacristy was the room where the Saint and her campanions studied; we can still see the confession box and the fald stool she used.

Hermitage of Nuestra Señora de las Vacas
Going along *calle del Granizo* we reach *plazuela de las Vacas* where we find the HERMITAGE OF NUESTRA SEÑORA DE LAS VACAS and although this place has no direct connection with the Saint we should visit it because of its peculiar interest. The strange name of this Virgin is derived from a miracle performed by some

19

cows, which, while their master was attending to his religious duties, ploughed the fields by themselves; this miracle again occurs in the Christian tradition and is very similar to the story of San Isidro, Patron Saint of Madrid. The magnificent bell-gable of the Hermitage and its beautiful retable make our visit worth while.

Convento de Santo Tomás

Continuing by *calle Huertos* and turning towards *calle Santo Tomás* we arrive at the CONVENTO DE SANTO TOMÁS, not far from the romantic ruins of *Sancti-Spiritus*. These ruins were once a Premonstratensian Monastery, founded by doña Berenguela's confessor, Nuño Mateos, in 1209; today it is a farm-house. *Sancti-Spiritus* was destroyed by the French during the War of Independence. The CONVENTO DE SANTO TOMÁS is one of the most beautiful buildings of Avila; it is in a tertiary gothic style having a noble porch with three arches. The interior is very rich with the tomb of Prince Juan, by Fancelli, a prodigious choir, and Father Ibañez's confessional where Santa Teresa used to kneel. The main retable, a masterpiece by Berruguete, is the most important work in Santo Tomás; there are three silent and secluded cloisters, a library, and a museum with a curious collection of birds and souvenirs from the Philippines. The sacred Host used by the murderers of the *Santo Niño de la Guardia* (1489) for their evil rites is kept, still uncorrupted, in the Sanctuary. This happening had a profound influence on the succession of events which finally led to the expulsion of the Jews.

Convento de las Madres

Going up *Paseo de Santo Tomás, La Ronda*, and *calle San Roque* we discover the CONVENTO DE LAS MADRES or DE SAN JOSÉ; this was the first foundation created by Santa Teresa. The first house was bought in secret on behalf of her sister Juana, don Juan de Ovalle's wife. Her brother don Lorenzo gave support to the foundation by sending fifty douros from India. Santa Teresa was as tenacious in everything as she was unfortunate in all architectural sense; she started the improvement of the building under her own direction; during the course of the work one of the walls collapsed, burying among the ruins her sister's only son. Teresa, taking the dead child in her arms, brought him to life again thanks to her miraculous mediation. The present building is a work by Felipe III's architect, Francisco Mora, who was a fervent devotee of the Saint; from it we can obtain a good idea of Herrera's influence; inside, in the *chapel of the Nativity* the remains of Teresa de Ahumada were kept from 1585 until the following year, when they were moved to Alba de Tormes. Several relatives of the Saint, among them her brother don Lorenzo, are buried in this temple. Her confessor Gaspar Daza is also buried here; he it was who conferred the conventual dress on the first four nuns of the Order. Julián de Ávila, her chief support in the creation of many foundations and her biographer; the mother and the sister of the confessor, doña Francisca and doña Catalina are also buried here; the latter was very much loved by the Saint. Her *relics* —a collarbone, the stone desk she used for writing, the belt of her dress, *Los Morales de San Gregorio*, written by her, a letter, the jug from which she drank, the flute and the rattle with which she amused herself, the ladder from which the Devil made her fall, the hazel-nut tree she planted by herself, etc.— are very interesting because of their authenticity.

Convento de Santa Ana

Behind the *Convento de las Madres* is the CONVENTO DE SANTA ANA or DE SAN BENITO as it was once called; in this convent Isabel la Católica was educated and Felipe II wore man's clothes for the first time; the building dates from the 14th century although it was improved in the 16th. At the foot of Bishop Sancho Blázquez's statue we can read some lovely verses in the style and metre of the *Cantar de Mío Cid*. In this Convent the Venerable doña María Vela "the strong woman" lived, a woman devoted to Santa Teresa, who died as a Saint on 24th September 1517.

Casa de doña Güiomar de Ulloa

Proceeding by *calle de Isaac Peral* after crossing that of Duque de Alba we reach the *plazuela de San Jerónimo* where we find the CASA DE DOÑA GÜIMAR DE ULLOA, Santa Teresa's loved friend with whom she lived during the days when she planned the improvement of the Order; she stayed in this ouse —also called DE LOS GUILLAMAS— at the same time that the Venerable María López, doña Güiomar's maid was living there. This two storey house with a renaisance porch and a mudéjar cornice today belongs to the Adoratrices.

Church of Santo Tomé

Following *calle Lesquina* we come to *plaza de Italia* where we must stop to look at the CHURCH OF SANTO TOMÉ, EL VIEJO (13th century); although this is an uninteresting building we cite it because it was there the Saint had to listen to a harsh sermon pronounced against her by a preacher wo possessed neither sagacity nor inspiration. Keeping its outer structure it has today been transformed into an Exhibition and Concert Hall.

Casa de los Deanes
In the *plaza de Nalvillos* which adjoins that of Italia, there is the CASA DE LOS DEANES a place without connections with the Saint but which is very beautiful and adorned by two groups of columns and lintel capitals, shields bearing the Chapter arms and reliefs with shields between supporting angels; the iron work of the balconies is rococco in style and on the baroque attic gable there is an old sun dial still marking the time. The Dirección General de Bellas Artes has made of it a Provincial Museum. Along *calle de los Leales* and through the door of the same name, we come back to the *plaza de la Catedral*, which we have already seen. In the basilica, the image of the *Virgen de la Caridad*, the Saint's chief inspiration, is worshipped. In the *church of San Vicente* which we have also already seen, the *rastro teresiano* of the Virgen de Soterraña is kept; it is said that the Saint took off her shoes in front of this Virgin when she moved to the ENCARNACIÓN.

Monastery of the Encarnación
This MONASTERY OF THE ENCARNACIÓN is outside the city, to the North; it was founded as an oratory by doña Elvira González de Medina in 1479 and received its present mission on 4th April 1515, this being the day when Teresa was baptised. The Saint received her nun's habit in this house on 2nd November 1533, and although she afterwards left because of her poor health, she came again later, being accepted definitely in 1537. In this house the Saint received visits from San Juan de la Cruz, San Pedro de Alcántara, San Luis Beltrán and San Francisco de Borja. Santa Teresa became the prioress of this convent; the chapel named after her stands on the site of her room.

Capilla de Mosén Rubí de Bracamonte
Passing under the walls again through the *Arco del Mariscal*, we come across the CAPILLA DE MOSÉN RUBÍ DE BRACAMONTE, well worth visiting, where there is, among other interesting things, a painting with a curious legend that says: "In charity beseech God's mercy for the soul of the noble gentleman don Diego de Bracamonte, who was beheaded in the *plaza del Mercado Chico*,

The mountains and the
Parador of Gredos

Casa del Virrey del Perú.
The courtyard

on Monday 17th February 1592 for having defended the rights of Avila...", etc. Don Diego de Bracamonte, *señor de Fuente el Sol* and *Regidor de Avila*, was condemned on a charge of opposition to the King's claims, who demanded a large sum of money from the city for war expenses. Mosén Rubí was don Diego's son. We continue along *calle de Bracamonte* as far as *plaza del Mercado Chico*, where there is the CHURCH OF SAN JUAN, a building which strongly recalls the past but which has no great beauty. It is stated that the Saint was baptised there; her parents don Alfonso Sánchez de Cepeda and doña Beatriz Dávila y Ahumada were parishioners of San Juan.

And finally, on the grounds where today stands the CONVENTO DE SANTA TERESA, which we saw on our first trip, stood the *house of the Saint*.

Could we add something more? Certainly, but have we come to visit the City or do we want to write its history?

It seems to us the former was our intention, rather than the latter which would be a very hard project. Don't you think so?

SOME SUGGESTIONS FOR THE EXCURSIONIST

For he who likes excursions —and we imagine our reader does— our countryside offers an interesting aspect in the four view points of Art, History, Sport or even mere tourism; giving us a little of everything. An old land —that on which we walk— full of romantic memories on one side and of an abrupt geography on the other, with high mountains and cold deserts, which qualifies it as unique. The country of Avila is an inexhaustible fountain of suggestions for the historian, and can be considered a recondite and perfect paradise for the sportsman, the skiier, the climber, the hunter and the angler. That peace and tranquility we find in the Aviles countryside, is yet another enchantment to add to the many a bountiful nature gives us.

The *Sierra de Gredos* —by itself— has more importance than that necessary to regard it as a mere excursion. Gredos is a whole world, as beautiful in Summer as in Winter; it exists in the high summits where we see curious examples of *capra hispanica* springing to view and it offers us, during the snowy months, some wonderful ski runs. A line of buses starting from the Garage Ávila comfortably links the city with the *Parador de Gredos.*

Apart from this excursion to Gredos the excursionist in Avila can follow us along the short itineraries we are going to offer him; they will afford him a wide general view of this countryside. We always start from the city and return there, so that the hurried or tired tourist can come with us on all our outings and choose the one he likes best. To avoid missing anything of importance, we are going to be brief yet comprehensive. Let's go.

First journey

Avila - Solosancho - with the ruins of the Iberic city of Ulaca - *Mengamuñoz - Puerto de Menga -* in the *Sierra de los Baldíos - Venta del Obispo,* where you can eat exquisite trout - *San Martín del Pimpollar - Parador de Gredos - Hoyo del Espino,* with the fishing preserve of the River Tormes - *La Aliseda de Tormes,* here is to be seen a beautiful retable in the Berruguete style - *Bohoyo,* on the left, with numerous blazoned arms on its façades - *El Barco de Ávila,* the native village of San Pedro del Barco, with the castle of the Dukes of Alba, remains of the walls and a beautiful bridge - *La Aldehuela,* in whose church we can see a gothic chalice and a pluvial embroidered in gold - *Piedrahita,* the native village of the Gran Duque de Alba, and where Goya spent some time painting; here we can admire a 13th century church. Until only a few years ago they prayed here for doña Berenguela's soul every Friday during Lent - *Villatoro - Ávila.*

Second excursion

Ávila, following the *Sierra de la Paramera - Navalmoral - San Juan del Molinillo - Navarredondilla,* beautiful little villages - *Hoyocasero,* with the *Hermitage of Christ* and three stone funeral urns - *Puerto del Pico,* from where we can enjoy a magnificent view - *Mombeltrán,* where is the palace of the Duques de Alburquerque, a church with wonderful images, the ruins of the *Convento de Santa Rosa* and the 16th century hospital - *Arenas de San Pedro,* set in a magnificent landscape, and offering for our admiration the castle of the Condestable Ruy López Dávila, the palace of the Infante Don Luis de Borbón, Carlos III's brother, a gothic parish church constructed towards the end of the 14th century and the convent where San Pedro de Alcántara died - *Candeleda*, in whose mountains we can still see lynxes if we are quiet and observant, a typical village, where they still tell the charming old legend of the *Virgen de Chilla*, which says that the Virgin, by her cries stayed the arm of a cuckold when he was about to strike his wife's lover - *Piedralaves*, also called "the flower of Tiétar" due to its pleasant climate - *La Adrada*, with the remains of a castle and a very rich church - *El Tiemblo*, with its famous bulls by Guisando at the parish boundary, and the ruins of the monastery of Jerónimos, where the nobles swore to depose King Enrique IV - *Cebreros*, famous for its grapes and posessing a notabe church by Herrera; a place to be reached by going along the magnificent *Alberche dam - Hoyo de Pinares*, an attractive little village, *Navalperal - Las Navas del Marqués*, set amidst spacious pine-groves where there is a castle, recently rebuilt, and the luxurious colony of Ciudad Ducal - *Aldeavieja - Ávila*.

Third trip

Avila-Gotarrendura, with reminders of Santa Teresa - *Arévalo*, once the prison of the unlucky doña Blanca and the birthplace of the Príncipe de Viana; there are several important religious buildings and a famous and crowded market - *Madrigal de las Altas Torres*, the famous village where Isabel la Católica and *El Tostado* were born; and where the Infanta Catalina and Fray Luis de León died; the ruins of its walls have great interest, as have the churches of San Nicolás de Bari and Santa María del Castillo; the Real Monasterio de las Angustias, the Real Hospital, the Arco de Piedra, the *Palacio del Tostado* and the house of the famous and unlucky pastrycook - *Cantiveros*, outstanding for magnificent Arab workmanship in the church-*Fontiveros*, birthplace of San Juan de la Cruz, with the superbly rich church - *Ávila*.

These three journeys have served to show us, be it ever so slightly, the whole region. The first, following the *Sierra de Gredos*, the second around the so called *Andalucía de Ávila* with its orange groves, its olives, tobacco, and cotton, climbing afterwards up to Las Navas; and the third about the flat Moraña so well known to Queen Isabel la Católica and the knights of her Court. These trips can show us all the magnificence of this countryside and initiate us in its spirit.

AVILA - MEDIAEVAL BAZAAR. CRAFTSMANSHIP

Yes, a mediaeval bazaar. Avila is, fortunately, one of the few bazaars of the Middle Ages that still remain. Its industry is still an art and secret, going from father to son, and its small, honest and neighbourly trading spirit still keeps the old and almost forgotten fragance of *toma y daca* ("give and take").

The industriousness of Avila, an industriousness one can neither see nor hear but sense throbbing steadily through the centuries, is remarkable for its simplicity and solid elegance, and for its honest sense of quality, Avila does not produce many things but the few it makes are very well made and with pride in their origin; this is the old artisans' motto.

In Avila and the surrounding country —you can find them all in the city itself— curious hand-made wares are available; of course they have no great intrinsic value, but they have a great emotional worth and a high suggestive capacity.

Perhaps the greatest charm of these things that we see everywhere in Avila, always calling our attention, exciting our curiosity and caressing our sensibilities, is to know they are like those that don Raimundo de Borgoña's captains, their wives and daughters might have used. It seems as if time was at a standstill in Avila's industry, and its products— simple, elegant and authentic— would appear to recall all the remote murmur of past centuries. Avila's industry —like the Sephardite Castilian language of Syracuse or Zagreb— found its appropriate tempo hundreds of years ago and thinks it is better to keep it unaltered; in this the Aviles artisans are probably right.

In the regions of Barco de Avila, Piedrahita, Hoyocasero —and occasionally in the city itself— we can still sometimes see women wearing the pleasing *gorra* of curled straw. It is a tall helmet-like hat adorned with different coloured wools, with an eyeshade from ear to ear on the front a small heart in metal on a background of material coloured according to the woman's condition. If she is a spinster the material is green, red for a

Casa de Velada

Church of San Vicente

married woman and black for a widow. It is curious to notice how often in their dress we see Castilian women wearing some sign indicating their position and condition. And the rather poetic adherence to colours indicating virginity, married state or widowhood is a curious relic from bygone ages. These hats are not difficult to get and they also make smaller ones for those who want the same souvenir but not so big.

The typical costume of this region has almost disappeared; that of the men, soberly elegant, is now only to be seen worn by a few old men who stick to it come wind or weather. The traditional female dress, rich in colour and pleasing to the eye, though less ostentatious than that of Salamanca, can still be seen on certain great occasions such as the Carnival in Cebreros, a fiesta which is outstanding in Avilesian celebrations.

The region of Avila being very rich in sheep, it is quite easy to understand why we can find wonderful woollen blankets of an insuperable quality. Those of Pedro Bernardo and Santa María del Berrocal, among other villages, are very thick and are striped in warm and brilliant colours. They are similar to those Mexican *ponchos* which perhaps have their origin in these old Aviles blankets.

Mule cart blankets, which are arranged like curtains at the rear, are as warm as they are decorative; and have the traditional peculiarity of showing, embroidered in different coloured wools, the date when they were made and the name of the cart owner's wife. This very individualistic sense of property carried to its extreme is a determining factor in the spirit of this region.

Beautiful blacksmith's work is done in the city —fences, crosses, andirons, grilles, door-gratings, balconies, knockers, hinges, locks, hig wrought nails, etc.— and the blacksmiths of Avila, who, however, never combined to form a powerful trade guild, have always been famous for the quality of their work.

The delicate filigree work in gold and silver from Piedrahíta (Ávila) —earrings, bracelets, pins, brooches, etc.— is like that of Toledo though a little simpler and of different taste.

The luxurious bookbindings, outstanding among which is the sober Castilian style, its engravings done by fire, are famous in Avila and amateurs and bibliophiles from distant places often have their most treasured volumes bound in this city. Speaking of bookbinding we should not overlook the careful, painstaking work that goes into the creation of mosaics made of various coloured leathers, remarkably beautiful effects being thus obtained.

27

Taxidermy, or the stuffing of animals, is also well represented in Avila by a kind and clever gentleman whom we dare name because he is a man who has not created an industry by his work. Antonio Guerras, has an almost complete collection of the whole fauna of the region and through his hobby he has brought an old tradition to life again.

Confectionery, wide in this range, delicately flavoured and made according to the old traditional recipes, is an art which is widely practised in the region, and one about which we will have more to say later on.

THE AVILESIAN CUISINE

Typical Avilesian dishes can be compared to the legendary egg of Columbus, they seem difficult to achieve at first but are easy when you know how. They are prepared with materials of the highest quality and so of course the dishes come out very well. Abulense dishes are liable to remind one of the well known recipe for the *sopa de piedras* (soup of stones): choose some small round stones from a river, wash them carefully and throw them into a cooking-pot in which you have already put two chickens each about two pounds in weigth, three pounds of good ham, two pounds of fine veal, some pork sausages, etcetera, season it carefully and once it is well cooked throw away the stones...

The cuisine of Avila is mediaeval, and savoury; reputed by popular legend to be capable of bringing the dead back to life, so rich is its composition. Abulense cooking is not compounded of frivolous delicacies but it is in itself an authentic gourmet's delight.

If we feel hungry, or more correctly, if we could assimilate such an ambrosial repast, we might select this succulent and rich menu.

An hors-d'œuvres of wild mushrooms —delicious mushrooms of which there is not a single poisonous variety— fried or grilled, freshwater crayfish and sausages.

Dried bean from el Barco with *chorizo* [1] from La Cañada or Navalperal; or a *cocido* of chick-peas from La Moraña. The

---

[1] *Chorizo* is a form of salami sausage made with pork and red pepper: it is very rich and piquant in flavour and the best of these particular sausages made in Navarre, in a little village called Cantimpalos.

beans or red pipos of Barco are perhaps the best in Spain and the chick-peas of other provinces cannot be compared with those of La Moraña. The sausages and ham of La Cañada and Navalperal are remarkable for their quality and fine flavour.

Trout, carp, and *panchos* from Gredos or from Adaja are firm of flesh and appetising to eat. The fish of the river Adaja which runs through the city have the strange quality of not putrefying after they are caught, it is only necessary to hang them up and they will keep in good condition for a long time. This quality is supposed to be due to the chemical composition of the river-bed.

One of the best dishes of Avila, and a very characteristic one, is sucking pig. The girl who serves it —you can find many places in Avila where a girl dressed in the typical costume acts as waitress— must cut it with an earthenware plate so that the guest can see how perfectly it has been cooked and how tender it is. This rite of cutting the sucking pig with a plate is a source of pride among the good cooks of the region.

Avila is also rich in game as the country gives us plenty of all varieties, each as good as the other. Partridges, rabbits, hares, wild boars which come from the country round Toledo and Cáceres and the she-goats from Gredos are of a very high quality. Game is abundant and, except in the close-season, we can always find it.

As we think our guest must feel his stomach somewhat full by now, by way of a change we are going to give him a good slice of veal. The veal of Avila is as white as paper and it is a food which cannot be bettered for giving to delicate and convalescent people.

It the guest dares —it is up to him— he can end with a ration of mountain kid, a very savoury dish and typical among shepherds; it is more than likely that the military virtues of the Aviles could be attributed to this succulent dish.

For dessert; *yemas of Santa Teresa, glories of Avila,* fried *huesillos,* sponge biscuits, rusks, fruit from the village of *Andalucía de Avila* and grapes from Cebreros; these are some of the finest and most exquisitely flavoured grapes in all Spain.

During the meal we must drink Cebreros wine, light on the palate yet full of body.

The bread the waitress serves us, made with wheat flour from La Moraña, is unsurpassable.

And so ends our characteristic Abulense meal; we do not suppose there is anyone who is still hungry.

THE AVILESIAN CHARACTER, LOCAL CUSTOMS AND TRADITIONAL FIESTAS

The Aviles is of a sober character, brief in his speech but capable of a wealth of affection; he is kind yet serious. without vanity, of a tired aspect and as good as his word. The women of the region are honest and discreet; and though they do not usually have a spectacular beauty they are sweet and elegant of expression. In short we could say that the people of Avila are just what we might hope to find, knowing the little we do of the city's history.

Perhaps Avila is the only city in Spain where one will never see a woman in the street who is exaggeratedly dressed or provocative in her gesture. The Avilesa knows that she has a certain position to keep and she maintains it with a constant and ever renewed zeal. Life in Avila is that of the Middle Ages in the middle of the 20th century, and probably this is its greatest charm and without any doubt, its force and prestige.

The Abulense fiestas, as become a city of such remarkable characteristics, are all of a religious character or at least are related to some religious event. About their significance let it suffice to say that they are celebrated in a city which, historically, has taken the surnames, *del Rey, de los Caballeros y de los Leales* and according to a popular expression it is known as *Avila de los Santos y de los Cantos*. The latter is an allusion to the little gravel we see in some streets and squares and also perhaps to the huge amount of stones they used to build the city, or even to the rocky ground on which it is built.

In Avila Carnival has almost disappeared; in fact it was never much celebrated. The spirit of the city did not harmonise with it very well. Carnival languished little by little and in the end it died a natural death. Among the villages of the region, Cebreros celebrates Carnival. It is a village endowed with an extremely mild climate, and is dedicated, as we already know, to the cultivation of olives and vines. Cebreros stands in a countryside more like that of Extremadura than of Old Castile. Carnival in Cebreros is very popular and noisy, it has a unique beauty and a particular richness. The entire population of the village enjoys itself in Carnival without distinction of rank, sex, or age.

The greatest fiesta in Avila is the one called after the Saint, from 8th. to 15th of October. Then there are dances, fireworks, bullfights and the amusing parade by the *gigantes y cabezudos*

Madrigal de las Altas
Torres. The Queen's room

Piedrahita. Church of the
Asunción

along the streets of the city to the music of pipe and drum. The pipe they use —the Spanish pipe— is not at all similar in appearance to that of Galicia or Scotland; it is an instrument like a small clarinet which gives us a sharp and lively tune, as delightful as a shepherd's chant. There are five giants taking part in the parade, each one represents one of five continents of the world; there are two *cabezudos*, male and female and each wears the typical costume of the region. The *gigantes* and *cabezudos* are followed by all the children of the town, dancing along the streets and having fun.

The pilgrimage to *Nuestra Señora de Sonsoles*, patroness of Valle de Amblés, is celebrated near her hermitage and it takes place on the second Sunday in October. It is very typical and the young folk of the village indulge in the *juego de la bandera*; this consists of dancing in front of the image of Nuestra Señora holding a flag in the hand and furling and unfurling it around the body in a delicate and agile movement. This fiesta is also called the *Ofrenda Grande* and the following Sunday the *Ofrenda Chica* takes place; this latter is somewhat similar to the former but not so important. On the last Sunday in June they celebrate the feast of the *Patronato de la Cofradía de la Virgen de Sonsoles*. In these pastoral sprees one can still see the hieratic and mysterious Castilian *jota*, and one can hear the folk songs —*aires*— of the countryside.

On the second Sunday in May a typical pilgrimage takes place near the *hermitage of Nuestra Señora de las Vacas* in the little square of the same name.

Holy Week in Avila is very silent and withdrawn and shows us a strong religious feeling. It has not the magnificence and outward splendour of other Andalusian and Castilian cities. Its most beautiful *paso* is that called *Cristo atado a la columna* by Gregorio Hernández which our companion already knows because we saw it in the *Convento de Santa Teresa*, the chapel where once Santa Teresa's room was.

In Avila there is a market every Friday of the year and plenty of sellers and buyers can be seen in crowded *cafés*. During Winter the Friday market —above all that of sheep and cattle— takes place in the Teso; during Summer near the *puerta del Carmen*.

The fair of San Juan takes place during the 21st, 22nd, 23rd, of June and that of San Gil on the 9th, 10th, 11th of September; these fairs are really great events in the city's life and people come from all over Castile.

During the first twelve days of August the old custom of *las cabañuelas* takes place, during which the weather-wise peasants venture to forecast what the following twelve months will be like. The first day represents January, the last December and between them, following their natural order, the months of the year. Many peasants still believe very much in *las cabañuelas*.

And that, my friend, is all we have been able to tell you, in this brief chronicle, of Avila. Now you know the city. Whether or not you come to love it, too, is not in our province.

PRACTICAL INFORMATION SUPPLEMENT

TO THE GUIDE TO

AVILA

HOTELS - RESTAURANTS - BULLRING - OFFICIAL CENTRES -
BANKS - ARTISTIC MONUMENTS - TRAVEL AGENCIES - TOURIST
INFORMATION CENTRES

HOTELS

H

★★★

PALACIO DE VALDERRÁBANOS - Pl. de
la Catedral, 6

H

★★★

PARADOR NACIONAL RAIMUNDO DE BOR-
GOÑA - Marqués de Canales y Cho-
zas, 16
PARADOR NACIONAL DE GREDOS - Gredos (60 km de Ávila)

H

★★

CUATRO POSTES - Paraje Cuatro Postes
ENCINAR - Carretera Toledo. Km. 137
REY NIÑO - Plaza José Tomé, 1

H

★

JARDÍN - San Segundo, 38
REINA ISABEL - Avda. José Antonio, 17

HR
☆☆

CONTINENTAL - Plaza de la Catedral, 4
LA EXTREMEÑA - Avda. de Madrid, 2
LA PAZ - Enrique Larreta, 1
EL RASTRO - Plaza del Rastro, 4

SANTA ANA - Alfonso de Montalvo, 2
SANTA TERESA - Carrt. Ávila-Villalba
LAS CANCELAS - Cruz Vieja, 6

RESTAURANTS

PEPILLO - Plaza de Santa Teresa, 10
CASA PATAS - Sta. Adaja, 25
EL SEGOVIANO - Vara del Rey, 4
PIQUÍO - Estrada, 2
LA TAURINA - San Millán, 1
ÁVILA - Plaza Santa Teresa, 4
EL ÁGUILA DE GREDOS - Plaza de San-
ta Teresa, 6
LA PERLA DE ORO - Vallespín, 24
ORO DEL RHIN - Plaza de Santa Te-
resa, 10

BULLRING

PLAZA DE TOROS - Paseo de San Roque

OFFICIAL CENTRES

AYUNTAMIENTO - Plaza de la Victoria, 1
GOBIERNO CIVIL - Av. del 18 de Julio, 1

BANKS

BANCO CENTRAL - Plaza de Santa Te-
resa, 10
BANCO DE ESPAÑA - Plaza de Calvo So-
telo, 1
BANCO HISPANO AMERICANO - Plaza
José Tomé, 2
BANCO DE SANTANDER - Generalísimo
Franco, 8
BANCO DE SALAMANCA - Reyes Católi-
cos, 2

2

ARTISTIC MONUMENTS

CATHEDRAL - Open all day (The Museum, Sacristy, Choir and High Altar can be visited from 11.30 a.m. to 14 p.m.)

BASÍLICA DE SAN VICENTE - Plaza de San Vicente - Visiting hours: from 9 a.m. to 13 p.m. and from 15.30 p.m. to 17 p.m. In Summer: from 9 a.m. to 13 p.m. and from 15.30 p.m. to 21 p.m..

CONVENTO DE SANTO TOMÁS EL REAL (Missionary and Natural History Museums) - At the end of the Paseo de Santo Tomás - Visiting hours: from 9 a.m. to 12.30 p.m. and from 16 p.m. to 18 p.m. In Summer: from 9 a.m. to 12.30 p.m. and from 17 p.m. to 19.30 p.m.

CHURCH OF SAN JUAN - Visiting hours: from 9 a.m. to 11 a.m. and from 17 p.m. to 19 p.m. In Summer: from 9 a.m. to 11 a.m. and from 18 p.m. to 21 p.m.

CHURCH OF SAN PEDRO - Plaza de Santa Teresa - Visiting hours: from 9 a.m. to 13 p.m. and from 16 p.m. to 19 p.m. In Summer: from 9 a.m. to 11 a.m. and from 16 p.m. to 19 p.m.

CONVENTO DE SANTA TERESA - Plazuela de la Santa, 4 - Visiting hours: from 9 a.m. to 12.30 p.m. and from 15 p.m. to 19 p.m. In Summer: from 9 a.m. to 13 p.m. and from 17 p.m. to 20 p.m.

MONASTERY OF LA ENCARNACIÓN - Just outside the Walls, to the North of the City

CONVENTO DE SAN JOSÉ O DE LAS MADRES - Calle del Duque de Alba. Visiting hours: from 10 a.m. to 11.30 a.m. and from 16 p.m. to 17.30 p.m.

THE WALLS - Can be visited from 10 a.m. with authorisation of the Tourist Office

CASA DE POLENTINOS (Academy of Military Administration) - Calle de Vallespín - Tourist Office authorisation required

PALACIO DE BENAVITES - Teresian Library, Museums of Popular and Taurin Art - Facing the Puerta del Carmen

PALACIO DEL DUQUE DE VALENCIA - (With Museum) - Calle de Lope Núñez - Visiting hours: from 9 a.m. to 11 a.m. and from 15 p.m. to 17 p.m.

CASA DEL MARQUÉS DE LAS NAVAS Plaza de Pedro Dávila

ARCHIVO HISTÓRICO PROVINCIAL (Historical archives of the province) With Museum and Library - Plazuela de la Santa

TRAVEL AGENCIES

VIAJES VELASCO - Generalísimo, 13

TOURIST INFORMATION CENTRES

Plaza de la Catedral, 4 - Free information about monuments, excursions, lodgings, etc.

ANDAR Y VER Collection. Guides to Spain

Majorca by Lorenzo Villalonga. **Iviza** by Arturo Llopis. **The Costa Brava** by Néstor Luján. **Barcelona** by "Jaime Miravall". **The Montserrat** by José María de Sagarra. **Tarragona** by José María Espinás. **Valencia** by Martín Domínguez Barberá. **Costa Blanca and Costa de la Luz** by José Luis Castillo Puche. **Madrid** by César González-Ruano. **Toledo** by Gaspar Gómez de la Serna. **The Escorial** by Luis Felipe Vivanco. **Avila** by Camilo José Cela. **Segovia** by the Marquis of Lozoya. **Salamanca** by Rafael Santos Torroella. **Burgos** by Fray Justo Pérez de Urbel. **Granada** by Francisco Prieto-Moreno. **Seville** by Rafael Laffón. **Cordoba** by Ricardo Molina. **Malaga and Costa del Sol** by José María Souvirón. **Cádiz, Jerez and Los Puertos** by J. M. Caballero Bonald. **Corunna** by Carlos Martínez-Barbeito. **Santiago de Compostela** by Ramón Otero Pedrayo. **Rías Bajas of Galicia** by José María Castroviejo. **Saragossa** by Luis Monreal. **Tenerife** by Carmelo Gacía Cabrera. **Gran Canary** by Carmen Laforet. **The Basque Country** by Ignacio Aldecoa.

ANDAR Y VER Collection. Aspects of Spain.

Bulls and Bullfighting by José Luis Acquaroni.
Andalusian Dances by José Manuel Caballero Bonald.